I CHOOSE Kindness

I CHOOSE SERIES

ELIZABETH ESTRADA

I CHOOSE
Kindness

DEDICATED TO B.L.

ELIZABETH ESTRADA

One day, I saw a group of girls laughing and **pointing**.
The new girl had tripped and dropped all her **things**.
As the new girl began to cry, the teasing didn't **cease**
Even when she said, "Don't laugh at me, **please**."

I joined in the laughing. I didn't know **better**.
The new girl tried to respond but only **stuttered**.
Emma, my best friend, walked up in **dismay**.
She said, "Let's be kind in all that we **say**."

I was surprised by my best friend, but also felt **shame**.
I wasn't accustomed to feeling so **lame**.
We ate lunch, leaving the other girls **behind**.
I didn't say much. I had a lot on my **mind**.

Emma told me about showing **compassion**.
How empathy and kindness were always in **fashion**.
Emma said, "We can show kindness in all that we **do**.
Simple things like sharing and saying thank **you**."

I sat down in class, thinking how I could **change**,
To be understanding and kinder felt a bit **strange**.
Soon it was recess, and I had a **plan**.
I drew a big heart in the **sand**.

I apologized to the new girl. "I really am **sorry**. I hope you'll see it in your heart to forgive **me**."
"My name is Olivia and I like to play the **trombone**."
"It's okay. Nice to meet you. My name is **Joan**."

We were now friends and that made me **happy**.
Because being mean made me feel **unhappy**.
On the playground, kids were playing **ball**.
Some boy tripped and took a hard **fall**.

I raced to help him and lift him to his **feet**.
It felt a lot better being kind than a **creep**.
When class had resumed, I wasn't so **glum**.
I knew being nasty was really quite **dumb**.

When the teacher needed help, I did it with a **smile**.
I picked up some trash that fell into the **aisle**.
I helped other students and passed papers **around**.
Everyone thought a new Olivia had been **found**.

When I got home, I helped make **dinner**.
I even wanted to make the kitchen **cleaner**.
I rang my grandmother to see how she **was**.
I helped my sister with her math, just **because**.

I feel happy to give kindness **away**.
I realize now it can change someone's **day**.
Once maybe a bully, but no longer **anymore**.
My heart is fuller than ever **before**.

I choose kindness. I don't like being **mean**.
As a kind, thoughtful person I prefer to be **seen**.
I'll be more compassionate and do good **deeds**.
Everyday, I'll scatter kindness **seeds**.

Being kind makes me feel good **inside**.
It's my secret power that I shouldn't **hide**.
I'll try not to judge or **tease**,
Treating others fairly with kindness and **ease**.

Beyond the Book

Sing a song to a friend.

Write a kind note.

Call a family member just to say hi.

Pick a flower and give it to someone.

Open the door for someone else.

Smile.

Give a compliment.

Make a kind gesture.

Start a gratitude jar.

Choose Kindness

Take a few breaths before answering someone.

Pick up your toys.

Bake some cookies for your neighbor.

Ask your mom or dad if they need help with anything.

Tell someone else what makes them special.

Help a friend in need.

Give a hug to a family member.

Pick up trash.

Dear Reader,

Thank you to my readers. I hope you enjoyed "I Choose Kindness." I spent a lot of time developing this book and series.

So please tell me what you liked and even what you disliked. What kind of emotion should be in my next book?

I love to receive messages from my readers. Please write to me at Elizabethestradainfo@gmail.com

I would also greatly appreciate it if you could review my book. Your feedback matters a lot to me!

With love,
Elizabeth

Made in the USA
Columbia, SC
05 August 2024